WE ARE AMERICA
the untold stories

portraits & stories representing
today's immigrants

Interviews & Stories by Students of Blackstone Academy Charter School

Photographs by Christy White
Edited by Bill Clarke & Susan Kaplan

Introduction by Stacy Joslin

Blackstone Academy Charter School
334 Pleasant Street
Pawtucket, RI 02860
www.blackstoneacademy.org

Project funded by Rhode Island Learn and Serve America through Corporation
for National and Community Service

CONTENTS

INTRODUCTION

Stacy Joslin, *Project Teacher*

This book is the culmination of almost 4 years' worth of work for a group of students at Blackstone Academy Charter School in Pawtucket, Rhode Island. After studying the first wave of US immigration in United States History, students decided that they wanted to write a book about the current wave of immigration, the wave that seems more relevant to them and their community. In the middle of this process, Deborah Reyes took on this book as her senior project. Her work and dedication were invaluable to the process and without her I do not think the product would be complete or look as good as it does. During the first phase of this process students interviewed over 40 immigrants living in central Rhode Island and created first person stories based on the interviews (Comments and thoughts remained unedited and may include incorrect grammar). Of the 40 interviews, 19 of them were chosen to be the stories of We Are America: The Untold Stories. With the help of a professional photographer, students photographed the people behind the stories.

I am lucky enough to work in a school where the students love to learn and are inspired to make a difference in the world around them. It is this culture that lead 2 seniors who were part of the first version of this book to realize that the work was not finished and asked to add to these stories. Gina Nuñez and Stephany Restrepo picked up where Debbie left off and lead a new group of students through this same process. And again, their work is the reason that this book is what it is today. They pushed themselves and their classmates to learn about this issue and impart this knowledge to the community through the interviews and writing. I am so grateful to have had the privilege to work with Stephany and Gina throughout this entire process.

Working with students and community members around this issue over the past 4 years has, without a doubt, been the highlight of my teaching career. I am amazed over and over again by the struggles, strengths and passions of the immigrants in the book. The students are equally inspiring, with their passion and desire to make a change in the world around them. Thank you to everyone who was part of this process, you have impacted me more than you know!

ACKNOWLEDGEMENTS

Deborah Reyes '08

Above all, we want to show our gratitude to the people who opened their hearts to us and allowed us to go into their past memories and write about them, thank you. Without each and everyone of you this book would not be possible. We have learned so much from your experiences and we wish you the best in America and in life. May your story continue on forever.

We gratefully acknowledge the generosity and support of Rhode Island Learn and Serve America through Corporation for National & Community Service, the grant that allowed us to complete this project. You believed that we had potential and because of that, we have created this book.

Stacy, thank you for supporting the ideas of students from US History so that we could create this book. You have supported our dreams and now we are seeing the fruits of our labors. Thank you for being the best U.S. History teacher, friend, and counselor. The U.S. History classes, I remember the brainstorming in Stacy's classroom last year in order to create this book. Thank you for all the conversations we had in order to start this book. We all have grown tremendously from last year to this year. We have created a book; we can do anything we put our hearts and minds to.

Christy White, thank you for helping out with the photography and layout of the book. Without your help, the creation of this book would have been a mission impossible to complete. Your creativity and dedication to this book is seen throughout each and every one of this book's pages.

Bill Clarke, thank you for stepping up to the plate and editing the stories. It has been a hard task to keep the stories true to the voice of the interviewee but the voice of the interviewee can clearly be heard through the words in the stories. Thank you.

The Immigration Project Class, who would have thought we would have the honor and pleasure to create a book. Thank you for all the time and effort you put into interviewing and writing the stories. It has been a pleasure and privilege to work alongside with such dedicated and talented people.

I'd like to thank everyone else who participated in this project. It has been a great adventure to work with each and every one of you involved. We started this project in a class conversation a year ago. Today, June 3, 2008, we have accomplished our goal of creating a book with the stories of immigrants in our community.

Gina Nuñez '10 & Stephany Restrepo '10

We first want to thank all of the people who contributed to the creation of this book. Without all of you this book would not have been possible. We want to thank you for being open to sharing your stories with us. Hearing all of your stories was extremely inspirational and we know that your stories will continue to inspire others.

We would personally like to thank Stacy Joslin for her immense help and support through the past 3 years. Without Stacy this book would not have been accomplished. We also want to thank her for dedicating so much time and effort to the Immigration Project.

The Immigration Project Class, it is such a pleasure to have worked with each and every one of you this entire year. We hope you have all been touched by the topic of immigration just as we have, and that you continue to educate others about this important topic. It has been honor to work with all of you.

Susan Kaplan, thank you so much for taking time out of your schedule to edit our stories. We really appreciate your help. You helped the process of publishing the book so that it could be done in a timely manner. We cannot thank you enough for your thoughtfulness and generosity in taking time to read and edit every single story.

Christy White, thank you for contributing your time to take pictures, and creating the layout of the book. Your creativity is truly shown within every page of this book. If it were not for you, we would not have had such amazing pictures. You brought these individuals' stories to life through your photography. Thank you so much.

We would like to thank all those who helped us accomplish the addendum to We Are America: The Untold Stories. Thank you to Debbie Reyes for inspiring us in our desire to continue this amazing book that has inspired not just us but many others in the community.

DEDICATION

As a class we have been inspired by many people throughout the journey of this project. Tam Tran is one of those people and has become one of our biggest inspirations. She gave us hope and motivation to follow our DREAMS, no matter the difficulties or the obstacles that we face through our lives. She was never afraid to speak out for what she believed in and inspired us to do the same. She impacted each of our lives in more ways that we can say. She helped us plan and organize a trip to Washington, DC where we marched with thousands of others in support of the DREAM Act. She taught our class how to lobby congress for what we believe in, even joining together in a meeting to lobby a US Congressman to co-sponsor the DREAM Act. Tam's impact on us is too immense for words to express, since she showed everyone that following your DREAM is possible. Although she is no longer here with us, she will continue to give us the strength and encourage to continue to seek justice for all! She will be missed by us and all of those she fought for and touched.

IN GOD'S HANDS
Miquel Lima
Guatemala
Interviewed By: Merari E. Lima

Interviewing my dad was very funny. I knew some of his story already but not all. When I see my dad it is like I am seeing myself in the mirror. We look alike especially our smile, the shape of our eyes and our attitude. I love my dad the way he is patient and tranquil always happy and in a good mood. Being away from him for a long time wasn't easy at all but thanks to God we are together again and this time no one is going to separate us again.

Coming to America wasn't easy at all. I had a daughter she was my first kid with my second wife. My baby was only one month old when I had to leave her in Guatemala. I had everything in Guatemala, we owned a house and a farm there was no need for me to come to America. But if I stayed in Guatemala I was putting my wife and kids lives in danger. My dad was a player who always cheated on my mom. For being a player and having to much land lead to his death. They killed my father for a stupid reason, a reason that wasn't worth it and I was afraid they would come after my family next. During my wife's pregnancy we had to travel from one place to another hiding and praying to God to take care of us.

A week before my wife gave birth I tried to cross the border, but I didn't make it. I went back to Guatemala for the moment that my baby was born. A month after she was born, I went back to try to cross the border again and thank God this time I made it.

While crossing the border our "el coyote" left me and my cousin behind. We were half way to the border. We keep on going, it was hard we had walk long distances but there was a time that I couldn't walk any more so we took a train the rest of the journey. God has always helped me; he has been there always for me when I need him. I have been living in America for eighteen years already. A year after my wife came too so we had to leave my little child in Guatemala. Eight years ago I brought my daughter to the U.S. to give her the opportunity to have a better life. I finally have my family together; it hasn't been easy.

I NEVER FORGOT WHERE I CAME FROM

Antonio Moreira

Cape Verde

Interviewed by: Deborah Reyes, Christopher B. Lopes, Latisha Amado

Antonio Moreira, the Portuguese teacher at Blackstone Academy, plays many roles in his life. A father, a teacher, a leader, a coach, he tells his story so vividly like it was yesterday. He never forgot where he came from and that has brought him a long way.

When I immigrated here, it was on August 19, 1991. I was just fifteen, at my age it was something exciting for me. Back then in Cape Verde, there was only one international airport for ten islands. Since the island that I am from, Santiago did not have an international airport I had to travel from Praia, to Sal where the international airport was, and then to Boston. When I came here, the first things I noticed were the smell, the size, and the people.

It was summer time and I was in the middle of Boston. I started missing my friends but I wanted to experience the American life. In Cape Verde, which is a poor African country, I heard about America from the movies and the people. It's considered the best country you can go to, everything is so big and there is a lot of everything. Being from a small island, you get to do a lot of neighborhood types of things. Being a young kid, I wanted to play, to be free and do the things you do outside. It was really frustrating to learn that you couldn't do that here; everyone pretty much stays in their homes. I barely saw my neighbors which was so different because in Cape Verde everyone knew everyone, it was a great family type of community. It took me a while to get used to that.

In Cape Verde I took language lessons, but when I came here I didn't know how to speak English. When I came to America, my sister took me to the high school and one of the first questions they asked me was if I spoke English. I said no, and they suggested I go to Jenks to work on my English. Although so much about life in America was different, I could still do what I loved, play soccer and basketball. I didn't know you could play sports and get scholarships. I played basketball for my high school and got recruited to play in college. Sports was a past time that I loved and it opened a lot of doors for me, for my education and continued athletics. I'm glad I came to America and finished my high school years here. It created a lot more options for me.

I'm glad my family moved to this country because this country can offer everything you might need in life but you really have to take advantage of the system. There isn't really anywhere else where I can go and get a good education based on sports. There are tons of kids who would love to come here and take advantage of what is being given to them but in my community, a lot of kids born here don't take advantage of what they have. It's easy for them not to take advantage of America and to fall into bad habit's. I took advantage of living here but I was careful to not fall through it's cracks, I never forgot where I came from. I feel that I am part of America but I don't feel American. Cape Verde was the country I was born in and I grew up in but this is where I work and where I live. Today, I still play sports, coach at Bryant University and Shea High School. I like to make a difference, a positive difference in someone's life.

THE AMERICAS
Cristina
Dominican Republic
Interviewed by: Priscilla McPhillips

When we interviewed Cristina she was wearing a light blue G-unit muscle shirt and gray sweat pants. Her hair was in rollers and she was acting professional.

I came to America from the Dominican Republic on April 13, 1989. I came here to improve my life and to start a family with my now ex-husband. I miss some of my relatives I had back in Dominican Republic. I also miss the warm weather and the tropical fruit's that my country has.

America is different from my country by many ways. First of all, the Dominican Republic is an island, the weather, the people and the landscape are very different. We don't have winter over there and we don't celebrate thanksgiving and other holidays. Plus the language, the music, the cultures and religion are all different. The hardest part about adjusting to American culture was the language, which took me a while to learn, but I got through it. I also had to adjust with the rain and cold snowy weather.

As a single mom I make my living by working in a day care center as a teacher assistant. In Dominican Republic when I was finishing my studies and I had a job as a secretary. It was really a part-time job and I was still living with my parents, but I enjoy my job here as a teacher assistant more because I love working with children. My daily routine is basically waking up, sending my kids to school, getting ready, going to work, coming back, and doing my chores... I enjoy every day as if it were my last. Many people see this land as the land of opportunities...like reaching heaven everybody has different dreams; it's like their expecting something from this land. My favorite part of American culture is the holidays and the sense of freedom that we have here.

I think immigrants have brought a lot of help to America by working in the factories and a lot more. Some people cause problems but not all of them. We have been a great source of work... Since they usually work cheaper because they don't have papers I really can't answer that question to the extent I would like to. If an immigrant I knew was coming to this country I would tell them to make sure they know what they want out of life because most people who come here they only come to find money and some people come for happiness but you can find happiness in your own country you just have to look for it. I mean why come to America any ways there are lots of other places to go and here some people just take advantage of you, besides I believe that we are all Americans because we all live on the same continent.

A SERIES OF FORTUNATE EVENTS

Cesar Gil

Guatemala

Interviewed By: Deborah Reyes

The whole time I interviewed my dad, he was laughing at his own story. He kept singing and telling jokes the whole time.

My name is Cesar Gil but my friends call me Tito. I came to America in the 1991. I came because I wanted to work for a couple of years. I wanted to work and bring back money to my homeland, Guatemala. My dream was to buy a motorcycle and ride back to Guatemala across all of Mexico and to spend time visiting places in Mexico.

When I came to America, I crossed the border walking and running. When we finally crossed the border, we were a group of 20 people including children. I got angry because there was an overweight lady that was with us; she couldn't walk and they couldn't help her. She was tired but the coyote, a person who illegally smuggles people across the U.S. border, left her there. She was left to be lost in the desert and we never saw her again. We never knew anything else about her, I don't know if she died or if anyone else helped her. I felt angry because the coyote didn't care about the people, all he cared about was the money. Of the 20 people, only 15 or 18 people got to the border and then they asked everybody to hide in the bushes. Somebody with a van was supposed to show up and pick up everybody but that was a big lie. We were hiding for one day and one night. The next day in the morning, agents from the border patrol was walking around the border with dogs and the dogs found a few of my friends.

I tried to run away but I decided to stop and they arrest me. I was at "El Corrolon" [the place where they took all the people that were arrested at the border], in Brownsville, Texas. I was there for three weeks and one of my friends bailed me out of "El Corrolon."

After that I met my friends in L.A. and was there for two or three years. In L.A., I found a long lost friend who was poor in Guatemala. I was very happy to see him again because he had a new lifestyle here. He liked to help the poor people and he spent his own money from his paycheck to buy food and clothes for the kids and to pay the rent. He died in a motorcycle accident. Knowing nobody in L.A., I wanted to go back to my homeland but before I went to my homeland I called some of my friends in RI and they asked me to come to visit them. I decided to come before going back to my homeland. I remember when I walked out from the Boston airport, when the gates opened I feel really cold because that day was winter. They asked me if I wanted to work and they found a job for me at a jewelry factory in casting. My intention was to be in RI for 2 or 3 weeks only but that never happened. Until today I have stayed in RI, I met my wife and now I have three little children. I am a legal resident of the United States.

I would tell all new-coming people to America, go to school and learn English.

WE'RE ALL AMERICAN
Nelson Agudelo
Colombia

Interviewed By: Melanie Gonzalez

When coming into the house I was scared, Nelson was very intimidating to me. But quickly I found out he was a very funny guy with strong values. With Spanish music in the background and his 3 grand kids playing in the other room, I interviewed him.

You have to recycle, you have to put new windows up, you have to keep your grass cut or you will be fined. They say America is land of the free but it is not. You have to follow so many rules, that's not freedom to me. Even after more than thirty years in America I still miss things about my country. I miss the weather and the culture the most.

I own my own house and I have to do what the city says or I will be fined. When I came to America 33 years ago, still a teen, I didn't know why I came. I came because my mom brought me here. I say we all come to America for the same reasons; a better life, better jobs, better everything.

Coming to America was worth it for me because I came here legally and it was easy to do things, the process was long but worth it. I adjusted quickly to life in America because I came here at a time when I was starting my life, I was a teen. This is where I met my wife, had my children and grandchildren. The worst experience I've had in America is looking Hispanic, it puts a black spot in your face, a sign to judge, it's not right to be racist or prejudice, but it happens. Some people don't understand we are all humans and all Americans. We all live on the same continent, the American Continent.*

* In Colombia, the Americas are considered one continent.

FAMILY REUNION
Tony Santos
Senegal

Interviewed By: Jaryde Spencer-Santos

As I interviewed my father, Tony Santos, I learned about his life. We were joking around while he was cooking Tuna and Rice for dinner. The interview went so well because we could talk almost like brothers in this setting.

My life in Senegal, Africa was enjoyable and care free. I was seven when my family moved to America. In Senegal, the weather was good and always the same.

I remember playing in the yard with my three brothers and one sister. We would sometimes go to the beach and swim long distances to a giant rock to dive off of. I really miss Africa.

When my brothers, my sister and I got off the plane in America in Boston, I remember the first thing I saw was snow. I was so amazed I never saw snow before (but then I went outside and I hated it). My mom, who I had not seen in three years, picked us up and brought us to her house in Rhode Island. We all cried and hugged, and so my life in America began.

Life was hard in America, especially since we didn't have my dad to help support us. One way I made my living was joining a band when I turned eleven, I was the keyboard player, we went to many gigs and I loved it I was living my American dream. In high school I learned about technology and computers. I met my wife Julie when I was eighteen, and now we have two kids.

I am thirty-seven now. My life has been hard, but I am trying my hardest to give my kids the opportunities that I never had, because in America, opportunity is right around the corner.

A SECOND CHANCE

Angelica Galindo Gil

Guatemala

Interviewed By: Deborah Reyes

I knew bit's and pieces of my mothers story and now I just wonder what would have happened to me if she hadn't been able to come to America the second time.

My name is Angelica Maria Galindo Gil. I came to the US from Guatemala on January 12, 1990. I wanted to come visit the "States" because I wanted to travel and visit my family who already lived here.

When I finally came to the United States, I decided to stay here and work in order to send my mom money. In the beginning when I came, it was very difficult because it was an unknown country to me, and I was alone here without my family. What I miss most about Guatemala is the customs and the food but above all was my family. When I first came to America, I worked for 2 years in a textile factory to help my mom support my 4 younger siblings.

In 1995, I had an emergency and I had to return back to Guatemala. I had the idea that I was going to stay and live in Guatemala, but when I actually got there, I saw that the situation over there was really difficult. In that time, I had no money and I went to Guatemala with a visa and stayed there for two months.

I decided to come back to the United States, I couldn't bring my daughter with me on the airplane because in Guatemala I was single and had no children. I had to ask a friend to take my daughter with him on the plane and that was one of the worst moments in my life. When I was on my way to the U.S., I had to change planes in Costa Rica. I wanted to see Costa Rica so I left the airport for a little while but when I came back inside, the Costa Rican Immigration detained me and started to ask me questions. They wanted to cancel my visa so I couldn't go back to the US. I knew God was going to let me be with my daughter again, she was already back in Rhode Island. After five hours, they gave me my passport back and all they told me was to have a nice trip. When I finally made it to the airport, I couldn't wait to be with my daughter again.

I've always liked to help people and the community. Now I am working in a program as a home visitor, teaching parents how to be teachers to their kids. I teach the parents a packet that will help their children learn how to read, write, and prepare them for kindergarten.

I have always wanted to go back to my native country with my papers. I got my residency on Dec. 23, 2005. There was always the possibility that I would not get my residency but I saw the hand of God and I got it in a matter of months after I applied for it. Today, I am working alongside with my husband and I'm trying to go to school again so I could get my associate degree. I'm happy in this country because it has opened the doors to my education and my life.

THE FORGOTTEN

Silvia Martinez

Colombia

Interviewed By: Lorraine Vergara

Silvia Martinez, mother of 8 and grandmother of 9, suffers from Alzheimer's but she still managed to follow through with the interview. She looked confused through the whole time but answered all my questions. She was wearing a small tee shirt and some shorts on the day of the interview. She doesn't remember the year she came here but she does know the reason she came which is to have a better life. She struggled in the interview with frowns and lost faces that she made but I managed to get some stuff out.

I know I forget things and I don't know why. I came to America from Colombia but I don't remember when. Things weren't going good in Colombia because we were poor so we had no food and we would go days without food. It was very hard for me because I had to support my family. I had 8 kids and one died and what made this situation even harder for me was the fact that my husband died of a heart attack at the same time.

I came to America by myself to have a better life for me and my kids. After a while of living here and working in sewing factory, I sent for three of my children. The rest preferred to stay in Colombia because they were older by this time and had lives and families of their own.

Everything was going good until my children here grew up and found families of their own. They don't really care about me anymore. They are too busy so they only come around once in a while. Except for one of my daughters, who I live with and takes care of me because I'm sick.

MY CHILDREN ARE MY FUTURE
Paula I Montes
Nicaragua
Interviewed By: Carlos Gonzalez

Paula, my mom, is a person with hope and love for her husband and their three children. When I interviewed my mother she sat down with me to explain how she got here, where she came from, and what is she doing here. A person that struggled for her life and children so they and herself can get a better life.

"Mom, mom, wake up I'm gonna be late to school to school!" This is my alarm every morning. The first thing I do when I wake up is feed my three children and take two of them to school. After that I sometimes clean the house, sweep the house, pass the mop, wash the dishes, and clean the rooms. I'm mostly a stay at home mom after what happened in my job a year or two. I'm used to work for a company that made eye protectors for the military but from working too much I got carpal tunnel syndrome on my hands and arm, and therefore cannot work in that job anymore.

I came from Nicaragua when I was young and came here because I had to feed my little girl and wanted a better life for myself and my daughter. Life in Nicaragua was pretty hard when I was pregnant. And life wasn't any easier when I had my baby. I left school to feed my child and had to work to get money but there are not a lot of jobs in my country. When I decided to come here, I went to Guatemala then kept going on to Mexico, I had to leave my daughter behind. I passed the border to get to California; I did all I could to come here from walking the streets, to hitchhiking, to paying people to take me to a place. While in California I meet my husband and moved to New York in 1991. My two other children were born there and I finally brought my daughter from Nicaragua and moved to Rhode Island.

I love life here more than back home because there are many more opportunities here than in Nicaragua. When I used to work I could get any job and they would pay better than if I work back in my country. And also my kids get a better education here than anywhere. Yes, I miss my family back home who couldn't come but sometimes you have to give a little to get a lot. I left my mom and sisters and relatives back in Nicaragua but here I have a husband that is a truck driver and makes good money, my oldest child graduated from high school and is now a medical assistant and is going to college, my only son wants to become a computer engineer and is a great artist, and my little daughter is still in middle school doing the best she can. My kids couldn't be where they are if they were back home.

BROKEN DREAMS
Hector
Guatemala
Interviewed By: Patricia Delgado and Jacki Cano
During the interview Hector was very relaxed. He was still in his uniform for work and he was really tired. He was very friendly and that made it easy to talk to him and learn about his story; he shared so easily.

My name is Hector and I'm Guatemalan. I immigrated to the United States in 1989 at the age of 17. I entered the US with the mentality of having a better future because back in my country it was bad, especially with the economy and security. I did not come here legally. My sister, Iris, myself, and a couple of people from our country crossed rivers and tall mountains to find a better life. I looked at this journey as an adventure.

My life in Guatemala was different. I used to play soccer three days a week. I loved playing soccer. I held a few jobs while in Guatemala, I was a machine operator, a carpenter and a month before I arrived to America I was a shoe maker. That was one of my favorite jobs I held, because I enjoyed making shoes and I had fun while doing it. My life here in America is very different. When I first came here I was told that once I started working I would get paid more then I used to for every hour. I never thought I had to pay rent but when I heard about 500 dollars a month I was happy. Life in America is very different; here you have to follow the laws, it's not acceptable to break the law. In other countries it is common to not obey the laws and have no consequences to your actions.

My average day in America I wake up, take a shower, prepare coffee, wake everyone before I leave because I make a lot of noises. It takes me a 45 minute drive to get to work. My occupation now is that I'm a supervisor at a laundry service; we wash hospital clothes. I have to deal with 65 people everyday and it's not easy. Sometimes I feel like giving up. My day to day work is a routine, I go to work, home prepare things for the next day, and then it starts all over again.

I believe that when you're by yourself you have to work hard but I'm here with my sister, she helped me out a lot. Being single is very difficult. Living here is a routine. You can get what ever you want if you work for it. In Guatemala no matter how much you work it's not the same.

STRUGGLES EVERYWHERE

Bello
Liberia

Interviewed by: Ali Baptista, Melanie Gonzalez, Deborah Reyes, and Lorraine Vergara

We were in a small office. You could tell that it was a sunny day outside since we could look outside from the window. He wore a brown leather coat. He was very serious while telling his story because it was a very emotional thing for him to remember about his past and what he had lived.

Bang! Bang! Gunshots were my announcements in school. Instead of hearing laughter I heard screams of scared people. I grew up in Liberia during the war. When the war first broke out in 1989 I was in my teens. That was a very hard point in my life; I was so young and had to see my friends holding guns, killing people, doing their drugs, throwing their lives away.

Half my childhood was spent running from bullets during the Liberian civil war. I saw and experienced things as a young teen that people shouldn't see in their whole lives; 8 and 9 years olds holding guns, teachers too scared to teach. All of this started because two tribal groups started killing each other and then it escalated to a war. There was no way around participating in it either; you had to defend your tribe to protect your life. But thanks to my mother who hid me and my siblings in the attic and bribed the soldiers with food they didn't bother us as much as the others, and that meant I didn't have to kill innocent people.

One of the worst things that ever happened to me was that I had to live in a concentration camp in Ghana, but at the same time it saved my life. Living there were the most horrible days in my life. Those scars will live with me for the rest of my life. I had to live there for a couple of years. It was so hard because I had no family, no support from anyone I was all alone. Since I was a refugee I had no job, and I needed money to buy water to shower. Life was hard. But my sister who lived in America would send me money even though she was struggling herself. I never really understood how hard it was for her to support us and herself at the same time. I thought in America there wasn't a struggle that you could just pick money from the trees and flush it. But then when I came here myself in 2000 I found out that wasn't the case.

I will never forget those memories, never in my life. I came here when I was twenty-one, life here wasn't anything like what I expected. And it was very different from Liberia. I love my country, having all the tradition, and family around, but here it's not the same. Everyone is always so stressed out about having to work and there's no time for family.

STRENGTH IN RESCUE

Denise Schorr
France

Interviewed by: Melissa Montoya

The silence, all eyes on her. Close to sixty students filled a classroom ready to listen to the petite women, the fragile voice, and the hurtful story of her past. Mrs. Denise Schorr, has many honorable titles such as mother, daughter, President of the Women's Culinary Guild of New England, but most importantly a Holocaust up stander and survivor.

Das Jude is German for "the Jews." In between the two World Wars, the Jews were the target of the Nazis and ultimately the head of Germany, Hitler. He was determined to wipe out all the Jews of Europe during the 1930's and 1940's. Unfortunately, my family and myself fit that category. I was born and living in Paris at the time of the occupation, but luckily my family was one of the few who were not deported to the concentration/death camps. Instead of hiding for my life like many other Jews, I was hiding in order to save the lives of many children whose parents had already been deported.

A family friend and a leader of the French Resistance, whose main task was to save Jewish children, introduced me to the idea. Through dark allies, during the day, during the night, in streets, still hiding from the Nazi's, from their parent's arms; children came, were found, and were taken from everywhere to be placed in shelters. Little did they know that what I was doing was for their benefit. Many children were saved from certain death, and imagine how many little souls would have survived if I had only found them quicker.

Liberation was what we had all waited for. I became a social worker and was helping to reunite lost families. I also was taking care of people who had been in hiding. Not only was the Liberation a great time for the countries, it was during that time when I met my husband, an American soldier who had been fighting in the war. We became the first Franco-American couple to be married in Paris after the war. After my marriage, I settled in the United States in 1946 and adopted five children.

Here in the United States I began to teach French cuisine and wrote a cookbook, My French Kitchen that was published in 1981. I later became the president of the Women's Culinary Guild of New England. My various titles bring me great pride, but out of them all, I am proud to say that I had saved many of little helpless souls as part of the French Resistance.

EVEN WITH DIFFICULTY IT WAS WORTH COMING HERE

Delia Agiular
Guatemala
Interviewed by: Jacki Cano and Angela Boror

Talking to Delia was very easy. She would respond to the questions quite well and actually gave more information than was asked of her. She was very comfortable and a joy to converse with. She just arrived home from work to do the interview and she started to cook dinner and make a fruit salad.

I have become a slave to the watch because I'm always looking at what time the day starts and what time it ends. In my country you don't do that. America and Guatemala are very different because of the different languages and also everyone here tells you what to do and what time to do it. I am from Guatemala, I immigrated in 1980 and I wanted to have a better life than what I had in Guatemala. I work as a chief clerk right now; that's the way I make my money.

Coming to America was risky for my family at the time. The process coming here has changed; a lot of people die trying to cross the border, girls are getting raped, kids and adults are dying, it wasn't this hard in the past. In America, some people say we have freedom but we only have some. We have certain freedoms but we don't have all freedoms. We have to follow certain laws and it's hard to adjust. I don't think it's all that free, especially in this time with all the stereotypes that are going on. Before it was so easy to fly to another state; it's not any more. You have to go through certain steps. They are almost taking your clothes leaving you naked to see if you have anything. Maybe it was free before but not anymore.

Americans shouldn't stereotype that immigrants just bring problems. They only see the bad things and not the good things that we have done for this country. There is a lot of Latinos fighting in Iraq but they don't see that. One time I had a confrontation with one of the kids that used to ride the bus with my kids I guess my daughter or son had a fight with another kid and the kid's mom called me an immigrant and to go back to your country, that they didn't want any immigrants around in this country. I told her that I was an immigrant just like her ancestors that had come from England, she got very mad and called the police and told them I was harassing her. The police was very nice and didn't pay attention to her. Also once I was buying the house, the lady that used to live on the 1st floor she said, "f$!# you ! Immigrant, get out of my house!" And she started to scream at me in front of the broker. Well that was a couple of difficulties I had here. Even with all this difficulty it was worth coming here because I wouldn't have what I have here, I wouldn't have it in my country.

WITHOUT US AMERICA WOULDN'T BE AMERICA

Jose Nuñez

Dominican Republic

Interviewed by: Gina Nuñez

Walking in, I found my father, Jose, sitting at our dining room table opening the mail he had received that morning. He was wearing dark blue jeans, a white short sleeved collared shirt and pair white sneakers. Walking in he greeted me in the best way and made me feel as comfortable as possible. We sat in his living room couches and started the interview.

I remember September 26, 1983 like it was just yesterday. Arriving in America from Dominican Republic, a young boy, 13, ready for a new beginning....ready for a new life. My goal as a student in Dominican Republic was always to finish my school and become a professional. Arriving in America everything changed for me. I didn't apply myself the best ways I knew I could have. Five years later, I became a father and a husband. My goal now is to have a better future for my family.

I've always had dreams since I was a kid but living in America, in order to make your dreams reality you have to work really really hard. Things don't come on a silver platter in America, not everything is as easy as we all think. My dream was always to be a pilot or a physiologist. Unfortunately I didn't achieve my goals but since America is the land of opportunities I still enjoy waking up every morning going to my job as a chef. I don't only do it because it's my job but, also because I have a passion for what I do. After all, I have been into the culinary arts business for a very long time so I did learn to get used to it and now I love it. Although I didn't accomplish my dreams and didn't become what I dreamed of, I still have a life that I am proud of.

America is a land where you can be whatever you want to be if you think positively and go ahead and do it, but it is still difficult. America can give you something but it wants something in return. You don't just get what ever you want.

Many people come to America thinking everything is going to be easy. Let me give you advice, it's not as easy as it sounds. It is not the land where you're going to get free money and everything is just going to come to you. You have to work very hard and become the best of yourself. You have to work for what you want.

All the rumors that immigrants have only brought problems to the US are all wrong. We, the immigrants, are a big part of the US economy. I don't consider myself American but I consider myself to be part of America, I feel I belong to America..... Without us America wouldn't be America. This is where I grew up, where I had my first love, where I had my kids, my home, fifty percent of my life I've been here. I feel at home.

FROM TEACHING TO BEING TAUGHT

Luzdary
Colombia
Interviewed by: Melissa Montoya

Filled with the smell of homemade lasagna, my kitchen has become a live journal. Luzdary is telling me her story, one that I have never heard. She is telling me of her life now, compared to the one she had in Colombia. Surprisingly there are striking similarities just like there are differences between her family and mine.

It's 7:30 and I am punching in at work. My routine work day starts at that time and ends at 5:00 PM day after day. After work I go to my English class where I attempt to learn the language. I come home very late in the evening to do the house chores and cook for my husband and myself. In my native country, Colombia, I used to be the one teaching and led a decent life; here in the United States I am the one being taught and my life is not as easy going as it was in my country. Now my life has become routine ever since I arrived in the United States 8 years ago.

Here I am a factory worker. In Colombia, I used to teach children with disabilities. That was my passion and to this day I still love little children. So many years of school and more than enough of practice in my profession have all been wasted. Flushed, never to come back in the "promised land".

Aside from all the struggles and the fact I don't have a career, America is something I always wished for. America is more secure, finding a job was easier, and the material objects are easier to get here than it would have been in Colombia. In Colombia once you reach the age of thirty, you are already considered too old to work. That is one thing I love about America, everyone works no matter how old you are.

In Colombia, I had a stable job and my income was sufficient to pay our bills. With the little money I make working at the factory, I am able to send money to my family in Colombia so they can have a civilized lifestyle, but also have a decent life here.

TAN DIFÍCIL
Yolanda
Guatemala
Interviewed by: Brianda Franco

I interviewed my Tia Yolanda one night in her small apartment. What shocked me the most was when she started crying because I asked her this question that reminded her of her father who she left in Guatemala. I feel so bad for her but I'm happy that she's here with me.

BEEP! BEEP! BEEP! Every morning I hear the same alarm telling me it's time to get up and work. The sun hasn't come out yet and I'm already driving to work. I work in this string factory that makes these strings that you put into cables; 8 hours of just standing there operating the machines. After work I have to go home, clean the house, and do laundry. I don't have time to even take a breath. The best time of the day is when I go to bed and then the next day it starts all over.

I come from Guatemala in 1995. I was in my early 20's and my mom wanted to come to America. My older sister was already here with her husband so we decide we would go. I came with my mom and my little brother and sister. We left in a bus and then we had to walk for two straight days. We couldn't stop because the migra might catch us. It was terrible; I was tired, hungry, and cold. The worst part was that we were all wet because we had to walk in a river. Then we had to cross a hot desert until we reach a city in Arizona. From there we took a plane to Rhode Island because that's where our sister lived. When we got there I was happy to finally see my sister and my first niece.

The hardest part was getting used to the cold weather in Rhode Island. In Guatemala the weather was always warm and sunny and here it was freezing. I really miss all my old friends, the weather, and the food. Hmmmm. My plans were to just stay here for five years and work a little. But instead of five it's been 12 years and I'm still here. I came here to be with my family, not to get a better life because I had that in Guatemala but I wanted to be with them because they are all I have. I'm happy that I am here but it is not easy at all. If you are going to come here you have to work very hard or don't come at all. I am proud of myself and my family and even if I'm living in America my roots will always be from Guatemala.

I CONSIDER MYSELF AN AMERICAN

Colombia

Interviewed by: Maria Benoit and Stephany Restrepo

Still sweaty from her run, I sat with my step-mom in her dinning room talking about her life. She seemed happy to tell her story even though the story was sad.

I emigrated from Barranquilla, Colombia. The life wasn't very difficult in Colombia but there was said to be better opportunities in America. I immigrated here because my parents had a working visa... And my parents believed that by coming here on a working visa would give my siblings and I better schools and a better life.

While in America my parents were able to work under the working visa. Time went on and the visa expired; they had to work a whole year without one. Throughout the year my mom supported our family by making curtains and other household items. She would sell everything she had made in different supermarkets each day.

I found it very hard to adjust to the life in America because the language and the culture were much different from ours. It also became even more difficult because I began to miss my family and friends more than I thought I would when I left Colombia. I knew I wanted to make something of myself, so I went to college and got my degree. I ended up with a good home and a nice job at a restaurant where I am currently the manager. My average day here doesn't really seem too interesting, I just go to work, go home and clean, and take care of my pets...

I've never really had a bad experience while living here, except I was once a victim of racism. I went into a clothing store and the lady working in the store followed me all around to make sure I didn't take anything. If I would have been of a different race such as white she most likely would not have followed me around. I think that she followed me around because of the stereotype people use against immigrants... It's not true for the most part because we are all immigrants no matter when we got here or where we came from.

As an immigrant from Colombia I consider myself an American... Not many immigrants I think consider themselves Americans. I consider myself an American because I enjoy everything about the American culture. I don't believe that there is one thing I don't like from the culture. One thing I would want another immigrant coming here to know would be to learn the language before coming and to assimilate without losing your own culture.

LA TIERRA DE OPORTUNIDADES

Gertrudis Rosario
Dominican Republic

Interviewed by: Carolina Rosario and Priscilla McPhillips

While we interviewed my mom she was wearing a spaghetti strap shirt and sweat pants. The interview took place at her job in the Sister's Beauty Salon. Gertrudis was really into the interview, she said it brought her back some good memories.

I lived in Dominican Republic, I came to New Jersey in 1987. My parents thought that if we came here that we would have better opportunities for my brother and sisters to further our education. I miss everything about my native county, the beach, the food, the friendships, the hotness in the summer, everything.

America is so different from the Dominican Republic. In America there are more jobs and opportunities then there is in Dominican Republic but more diversity. It was worth coming to America because the opportunities make it easier for one to progress and raise a family, but it's a lot to get used to for me.

I came to America to study and finish high school, when that was accomplished I tried many different professions and finally found the one that I am still with today. I started in a clothes factory, then to a beauty salon, a carton/box making company, I started my own restaurant business, but it did not work out so I went back to the carton/box company. When I moved to Rhode Island, I went back to working at a beauty salon, finally opening my own beauty salon.

A typical day starts out with me waking up in the morning and taking my three beautiful daughters to school, I come back home, cook, clean, shower, and then go to work. America has been good to me, it truly lives up to the title "The Land of Opportunities." Although it has been good, there have been bad times; my divorce would have had to have been the worst.

There has been a vicious rumor going around that immigrants have brought problems to America, this is not true. Immigrants have brought benefit's to this country because this is the land of the immigrants. If there were no immigrants then there would be no America because the majority of the population is immigrants. America has changed my views and goals, the amount of jobs and opportunities are endless, America has given me the opportunity to achieve my dreams.

RUNNING FOR MY LIFE

Sokhon Sam
Cambodia
Interviewed by: Deborah Reyes

Sokhon is the mother-in-law of my Spanish IV teacher. As she told her story, I could notice there was sadness in her voice, while reminiscing about the past. She is the voice for all the Cambodian individuals who lived through the Communist Khmer Rouge's rule.

My name is Sokhon, and I came to the United States in 1980. I came to the United states because I fled from Cambodia. I left Cambodia because I lost a son and I knew if I didn't leave I would be dead.

In Cambodia I lived in a concentration camp, Cambodia was dictated by Pol Pot and the Khmer Rouge. They didn't give us any food, I only got a teaspoon of rice for me and my son once a day. I worked for nothing. Women worked in one field and men in another. You worked from like 3 A.M. to 12 P.M. Sometimes I didn't know if my husband was alive I didn't see him for many weeks. I remember, I would go to clean the cloth [diaper] for my son before work but that was all. I remember, Pa my husband, found a crab while working in the fields. He hid it under his foot so he could to give it to my son, he risked his life if the soldiers found the crab they would have killed him. There was no food and he chose to feed his son instead of himself. He snuck it into my house so I could give the crab to our son. I couldn't breast feed him because I wasn't healthy myself. When he was sick, I took him to the medics. The medics were old Cambodian women, they weren't trained and they injected him with something and he died. When my son died, I wanted to bury him in a clean place. When people die in the camps, they just took the bodies and threw them on top of the other dead bodies. My son died when he was three years old and the government would only give us a bowl of rice. He died of starvation. Pa moved the bodies to put my son in a clean place. I walked away and I had to return to my daily life in the fields.

I moved to Thailand at six months pregnant with my third son. To get to Thailand, I walked with Pa at night, and I slept under trees. We couldn't walk during the day because if the communist soldiers saw us, they would kill us. The communist kill a lot of people, they had no reason to kill us, they just killed us if they thought people were better than them. I was afraid every night, afraid that I would get killed.

In Thailand we stayed at a refugee camp. Pa filled out an application for refugee to the U.S. After he filled out the application, we stayed in Thailand for one year. My second son was born in the refugee camp and I also became pregnant with my third son. After we finally left Thailand, we stayed in Alaska for one night and then we arrived in Mobile, Alabama. Two weeks after we got to Alabama, my last son was born.

A DREAM FULFILLED

Freddy Osorio
Colombia

Interviewed by: Sebastian Osorio

The interview took place at home. As I begin to bring up these questions during the interview I felt odd inside because I had never discussed this situation with my father. Although I felt shy during the beginning he was very comfortable while answering questions and had very strong opinions

My dream was fulfilled. That's what I thought when I first came to America. But what I didn't know was there were challenges awaiting me. In 1989 I flew to Japan, assigned to fix parts on Kawasaki Motorcycles. I flew from Medellin, Colombia to Mexico City, Mexico to Los Angeles, California to Honolulu, Hawaii to Seoul, South Korea to Osaka, Japan. Coming back from Japan to Colombia I passed the second time through Los Angeles. Los Angeles is a big beautiful city where I noticed and realized that there were many opportunities to work. Three years after I arrived in Colombia I decided to come to the U.S. I came to the U.S. as a visitor arriving to meet with a family member. Of course, like most who have arrived newly to this country I had many difficulties including mostly the language. It was also difficult job-wise andit was always difficult to maintain a job in this country.

After six months my tourist visa had expired indicating that I had to go back to my country, but I didn't and from that point I became an Undocumented Immigrant. In 1995 I applied for residency and then three years later I applied to be an American Citizen and I got it.

I believe this is the land of opportunities but what I am against is deportation of the Undocumented Immigrants. I believe they should be granted citizenship because, there are many documented immigrants today that were Undocumented and have had great strides in the United States, like athletes, movie stars, astronauts in NASA, and famous doctors that have dedicated their lives to this country to make themselves and the United States better.

I AM SOMEBODY

Iris Cano
Guatemala
Interviewed by: Jackie Cano

Along with her confidence and her beauty, I couldn't help but admire the joy that came from my mother as she told her stories. As she told her stories she would get up and make it into realization. Even if the story was sad she still managed to keep a solid smile.

On January 22, I left with 350 dollars and with 22 others. It took me about 17 days to arrive to R.I from Guatemala. For some, coming here might have felt like an eternity or a tragedy, but for me it was an experience I will never forget. Crossing the border was an adventure. From country to country, from rivers to mountains, from trailer trucks to bus stops, I loved every single piece of it. Perhaps, it was because I never really had much freedom.

Growing up, it was as if I was the mother to my brother and two sisters. I remember every day before school I had to get everyone bathed, dressed and fed before I ever got to help myself out. I always had to rush home and make sure there was food on the table for my dad and that was pretty much the only time I ever saw him. Somehow while managing school, home, and kids, I still managed to join gymnastics. Every time I had a performance I always looked to the bleachers and saw no one from my family there due to too much work. I knew that I did not want the same for my kids; I wanted to be there for my children. I knew I had to get away from the life I had been living; my mom knew too. My dad didn't want to let me go but being the woman I am, I refuse to be caged down. As soon I became 18 I snuck out to the voyage to my freedom.

I remember hiding in Orange Crush trucks, which were already set up for us. If I wasn't on a truck then I was climbing mountains. I remember my first meal on American soil came out of a vending machine. It all seemed like a movie to me. I was starving and I knew I couldn't keep quiet much longer, with hand gestures and Spanglish I made it through. I made it through and finally after 16 years of struggle, I became a citizen. I am now happily married and have three beautiful children, and you can find me on those bleachers.

IN AMERICA I FEEL AT HOME

Diana Ortiz

Colombia

Interviewed by: Brittany Ortiz

I interviewed my mom, wondering what she had been through coming to the United States. I was able to find out; America is like her home.

I was 13 when I first came to America. Arriving in America from Colombia, at 13 years old, ready to start a new chapter in my life. I came with my mom, 3 brothers and 2 sisters. We came because my father had papers here, after working for a company that sponsored him. I didn't know much English when I first arrived here; it was difficult not knowing what others were saying, or not being able to speak English. As a young child I always wanted to pursue in the medical fields. Coming to America for the first time was an eye opening experience, new places, different people, new society and challenges. Even though my dad was here, I was still nervous to come here. A couple years later, I became a mother and wife. I did everything to support my family and do the best that I could.

I had dreams to become a medical assistant, but coming here changed that at first. I worked in a factory for 20 years, making jewelry. Once the factory closed I didn't know what to do with my life anymore. With the courage of my amazing sister, I enrolled myself into college. Once I graduated, thank god I found a job in Lincoln, RI, as a medical assistant. It was hard, after 20 years to go back to college. I felt as if I needed to do it.

People think coming to America your life would change for the better. It might and it might not. I had difficulties in life coming to America. You don't know what to expect once you come here. It's a new experience, new place, all different kinds of people etc. everyone in America should have the rights as an American. You might not have all the rights as an American in life, but take advantage of what you have in this country. I don't know what I would do if I was to get deported back, I would leave everything here, my family, kids, job etc. America was something way different then Colombia. In America I feel at home.

THE IMMIGRANT, GOAL

Jose Dos Reis
Cape Verde

Interviewed by: Tatiana Reis

I know you struggled through this interview and tried to hold back the tears. I know it was hard for you to tell me this story but I am proud that you did. Thank you for coming to America and making my life better than it would have been. Thank you for being there for me and always telling me to look into the future. I love you.

I was sixteen years old when I decided to leave Cape Verde and become a sailor on a German ship. And it was on that ship that I had the opportunity to travel the world and see all these different countries. I traveled all around the world from Mexico to China. I had the opportunity to experience all these countries and at the end of the day I knew America was the country for me. Out of all these countries I knew America was where I wanted my children to grow up in. Even though they weren't born yet, the goal for me was to create the best future I could for my family.

When I decided to come to Rhode Island, I was already writing to my girlfriend about my decision. I arrived here with a visa and soon married her. The United States wasn't all that different for me because I was already used to the European life style back in Germany. But I was surprised that everyone was so into basketball here because back in Germany it was unpopular. But I was glad I finally got here and was one step closer to reaching my dream goal.

On December 5, 1992 my goal was reached. My son Bruce Jose Dos Reis was born. My first American born child! Finally my child can have the future and the opportunities that he never had when he grew up. Then on October 5th, 1995 I was blessed again with my second American born child Tatiana Ana Reis. I thank God each day that He blessed me with two wonderful children and that He helped me reach this goal. America was a country that I always wanted to be in. Even though I traveled around the world as a assistant engineer on a ship and being able to experience all these different countries and cultures, I realized there was no country like America. And today I'm very proud to be an American citizen.

TO GOD WE ARE ALL THE SAME

Anonymous
Colombia
Interviewed by: Cristian Giraldo and Diana Giraldo

We sat there with him and he seemed nervous to be there and telling me such a private and confidential story of his life.

The decision was not mine. It was my parents who had decided to send me to live to the United States with my aunt and my brother. My brother had gotten all his documentation legalized thanks to my aunt, but when I came here she wasn't able to do the same. I arrived to the United States at the age of 11 coming from Cali, Colombia, leaving behind all my loved ones and only bringing a picture of my family. That was the only way that I would beable to remember them.

My brother's facial similarities with me gave me the opportunity to come to the United States using his passport. I had applied for a tourist visa but was denied. Therefore, my only option left was my brother's documentation. My brother and I look so much alike that people still confuse us. I was able to get his documentation, and since he was legalized he was able to come and go as he wanted.

When I arrived to the United States I had to surpass many struggles regardless of my age. I had to first go to school and try to finish my high school career where I suffered due to the language, and college was not an option for me after high school. Once I was old enough to work, I started working forgetting about school and trying to support myself and my aunt who is a sick woman. Walking or riding my bike was the only source of transportation, I had to go to work rain, snow, or shine I had to be a responsible young adult.

Today I am 28 years old and I still have no proper documentation to be "good enough" in this country. I'm a person who has done nothing other than work and try to better my families in Colombia and mine with my beautiful girlfriend. I wish that I can go back to my glorious country where I was only able to live for 11 years and have the possibility to come back to the country of opportunities. I hope that Barack Obama approves a method of legalization in the United States because I feel less than everyone else I am judged because of my status, instead of taking a minute to see how I really am as a person, student and worker. To God we are all the same.

WHERE WOULD I GO

Tam Tran

Unknown

Interviewed by: Diana Giraldo and Cristian Giraldo

We sat at the Starbucks on Thayer St. where she seemed excited to remember and share her past with us especially since she knew who we were and the school we came from.

I have no place to call home. I have lived in Germany and America, but my parents are from Vietnam and yet none of these countries consider me part of them.
My parents are Vietnamese and escaped from the Vietnam War and were picked up by the German navy and taken to that country. That's where my brother and I were born in Germany.

I was six when we moved to Southern California. I never knew why we moved to America until I asked my parents. It's complicated to say exactly what caused us to move. Many of the reasons were political views and family reasons. "I remember my dad telling me once, "We have to go back one of these days." I said NO I don't want to go back because deep inside I was scared. After a couple of years here I didn't speak German anymore and I had never been to the land that my parents were from.

When I looked at all the struggles I had to face in the U.S I realized that the psychological problems were the hardest to face. I was positive that I would get deported at any moment. It was before I finished high school when I realized that being an undocumented immigrant was a big deal. I wasn't able to get a driver's license and instead of going to college, I had to work since I wasn't eligible for financial aid or loans.
When I look at the immigration situations I notice that it's not fair how millions of people are forced to leave the country and go back to their home lands when all they wanted was to make the best of what we have. It got me really upset and angry when we didn't have access to higher education or jobs. That is what I'm working on and have worked on for the past ten years. I am now part of the Brown Immigrant Right Coalition (BIRC), co-founder of Student Immigrant Movement of Rhode Island (SIM) and one of the founders of Coalition of Advocates for Student Opportunities (CASO) which are groups at Brown University that help undocumented students go to college. Being able to work with these groups has given the hope that we would be able to pass legislation at the national and state level in order to help students go to college whether the colleges are private or public.

Right now I am very grateful for the most important thing I have brought with me; that would be the culture my parents taught me from Vietnam.

*I personally want to dedicate this book to the work and memory of Tam Tran. You will be missed!! - Diana Giraldo

Photographer Unknown

JOURNEY OF OPPORTUNITY
Maria Restrepo
Colombia
Interviewed by:Stephany Restrepo and Gina Nuñez

As we sat on the couch interviewing my mom, she was doing "joyeria" and watching Telemundo. She seemed more than happy to share her story with us of how she came to the U.S. Even as she spoke of her struggles traveling through Central America to reach the United States she kept a smile on her face.

I left Colombia on March 3rd, 1990. It took me about a month to arrive in the United States. I came through "el hueco", through Mexico and all of Central America in a bus and sometimes in a train. It was a rough trip. When we were in Mexico they gave us a big cup of coffee to see if we had drugs inside us. If we had drugs inside of us we would throw up the coffee after drinking it, but since we didn't have drugs and were very hungry we would drink all the coffee and they kept giving us more coffee. After this we were stopped in another part of Mexico by the cops because we couldn't remember the address of where we were supposed to say we were staying at. They got us off the truck and left us in the middle of Acapulco, and then a Colombian man found us there and took us out of Acapulco. Meanwhile, my family in Colombia would call the coyote and he told my family that they had us at this luxurious home on vacation but that was all a lie. In fact we were starving and they had stolen all of our things.

We would spend up to 15 days wearing the same jeans and shirt, and everyday we had to wash our undergarments in rivers to be able to wear them. It was a long and tough trip. For that whole month I didn't know anything about how my family or my husband was. Thankfully when I finally arrived in Los Angeles I was able to communicate with my family back in Colombia and my husband Juan. My husband sent me money so I could buy clothes and a plane ticket to get to Rhode Island where he was.

I would never advise anyone to go through "el hueco" as I did, because it can be very dangerous. Sometimes the coyotes try to rape you, or they tell you that if you sleep with them they will get you to the United States faster. Although I went through many obstacles to come to America, it was worth it. I have been married for 20 years and I have three wonderful children, and I find myself very happy to be in this country and I thank God for giving me an amazing family and for letting me be in a country with so many opportunities.

WITH NOWHERE TO GO AND NOWHERE TO BE

Carlos Lopes /Calu Bana
Cabo Verde
Interviewed by: Adelsandra Lopes

I have never known how much music had a significant impact in my fathers' life or being a great facilitator to most of decisions he had taken; until I sat down to conduct this interview. In fact, all I learned throughout this interview is that without music, and education, my father's life would not be as remotely as what it is today. I'm proud of him and proud to say he is MY FATHER! I love you.

At age 29 I was ready to say good bye to friends and family to start a new life in America, with a steady plan: to get a better life, better education and have a couple of music cds recording, since Cape Verde at the time we did not have any recording studio. I've always dreamed to come to America, and my journey to America was not easy as I thought, because I had no family, didn't know anybody, and to make matters worse I was an undocumented immigrant.

I still remember, May 29 of 1989, the day I arrived at Boston Logan Airport, a great place to use as a hub if my journey only involved an overnight stop, but unfortunately Boston was my destination. I sat there all alone. Nowhere to go, witnessing an enormous traffic of people coming and going to pick up and drop off their loved ones and I said to myself: gee it was just 10 hours ago that I left my poor Island (Santiago) surrounded by family and friends, and here I am with nowhere to go and nowhere to be. Difficulties presented itself right there and my life in America began. My first year was tough; I had to adjust to the culture, cold weather, food, driving, career change, and racial discrimination in order to survive. Therefore, I missed pretty much everything from Cape Verde, the good weather, the beaches, my mother's good meals, my family, and my culture. Thanks to God I was a singer, and I had a chance to join a band and had many gigs that served as part of my living.

During my second year, I met my wife Ana; she encouraged me to go to school, get a better job, my life turned around, and it could not be any better. Today, I can proudly say that a man who came here 20 years ago as an undocumented immigrant with nowhere to go and nowhere to be is an American citizen with a computer engineering degree from Wentworth Institute of Technology, has recorded more than 5 music CD's, and has the most beautiful family in the world.

Love you America, and all I had fantasized about you when I was back home became a dream come true.

THE RIGHT WAY

Adriana
Colombia
Interviewed by: India Young

This interview took place in Dexter Credit Union, where Adriana works with my mom. As I asked her these questions she paused and looked at me and then answered.

I was born in Colombia , and arrived here with both of my parents and four sisters. It took 15 years for us to arrive here, with a green card. I was seventeen when I first arrived here. In the beginning it was hard to come here, because you didn't know the language, so it's like you are afraid to talk to people I don't know what the people are going to say to you, and sometimes they make fun of the way I speak. I didn't pay it no mind when they made fun of my accent. Why did I come here, well she said looking out the window aside me, we came here like every other family, for a better life, and just like some of the families that come here we succeeded and my parents made a good life for me, and my sisters.

I feel bad for the people that come here to have a better life. I think that people should come with the right documents, and the right paper work, and you should come that way because you should not have the unfair option of being deported, and I feel bad for people that can't get here, because this is a free country. Some people just want come here, make money and send it to their families. We went back to Colombia three years ago, with my husband and daughter, but we just go for vacation and to relax. Now that my family and I have the money; we can go back to our country and see all the nice things that they have there.

LEFT BEHIND

Eliana Castro
Dominican Republic
Interviewed by: Paola Arroyo

I interviewed my US History student teacher Eliana in the afternoon during Immigration class. I was surprised about how much she had gone through without her mom. While I interviewed her it became clear how much she had left behind in Dominican Republic.

My heart was broken when I was raised without my mom for five years. She had married an American citizen, who was going to help her come to the United States. In the middle of all this she found out she was pregnant with me, so she had to give me his name. When I was seven months old she had to leave me with my grandmother to come to the US. Because I was so young, I had no say in this, and I was left in DR without my mother.

For years my mom continued to go back and forth between DR and America. I continued to live in DR with my sister and some cousins, at our grandmother's house. It was a nice childhood; we lived on a big farm. Every day we would walk play outside, walk to school and walk to the beach. We had enough food and good clothes, mostly because my mother sent money and packages.

When I was about five my mom got me and my sisters visas. She flew down to DR, and we flew back to Boston with her. When I first got here it was difficult because everybody knew how to speak English except me. It was pretty easy to learn English because I was so young. I also had a hard time adjusting to cold weather because I was used to living in warm weather. Back in DR everybody knew each other in my small town, however in America, no one knew anyone because it was so big. I was told not to talk to strangers and I had to be careful crossing the street. My life changed because I couldn't understand anyone or play outside like I used to.

I would like to go back to DR and visit more often. My family and I do get to go back but it is hard because it is expensive. My dad and six of my siblings are still there. It was very different before last year because we used to visit when my grandmother was alive. Now we're all scattered around the country. I wouldn't want to stay there for good. I like living in the US because there are opportunities available like financial aid. You can go to college if you want, you can get resources and programs and that's why life is so different in this country. There, the power goes out a lot; people lose their jobs if they vote for the wrong person, and there are so many big problems that the government doesn't want to or know how to handle. The quality of life is different in the United States.

I WANT TO SEE MY FAMILY

Anonymous

Colombia

Interviewed by:Diana Giraldo and Cristian Giraldo

We were in the living room of her home. She seemed a little uncomfortable but ready to help give me the story. She was wearing a pair of jeans and boots and told me that the hardest part would be saying things that would cause crying..

"You have been denied your VISA to travel to the United States." That is what they told me when I went down to the airport in Bogota, Colombia. I was so sad and I thought that everything I had done to be someone better and be able to see my mother again was gone. I called my mother and was so sad that I couldn't help but cry myself to sleep.

My mother left when I was 10 years old. She went to a new country in order to let her kids have a better future. My father didn't want me to go to another country where I wasn't going to see him. I was 14 in a country where I had my family and friends but didn't have my brother, sister or mother. When I had the opportunity to come to the United States I took it with no doubt. I went down to the airport and got denied my visa. I called my mother to tell her the bad news. They knew a friend who wanted to get my family reunited. They offered to give me their last name to see if I would be issued a visa. I was able to get my passport and was finally able to obtain my visa to come to the United States. When I got here, I changed my last name back to my real one.

When I arrived everything was so different but my happiness was being able to see my mother, my sister and my brother. I came and went to high school like a regular student would. I had many difficulties while I got older: not being able to have a job, having no way of obtaining a license and the frustration of not being able to go to college. These frustrations were because of my immigration status. My immigration status was the only thing that kept me from getting my license, having a job and going to college for less money. I was always challenged with different customs and surprises, but I never lost the most valuable thing I brought with me. I was able to keep my customs and culture that I had brought with me from Colombia.

When I look at the immigration laws and see what they have done to me, I feel discriminated. I wasn't able to live like a regular teen my senior year of high school, I had the struggle of worrying about college and being able to attend. If it was up to me I would change all those laws that punish young teens and children who didn't choose to come here undocumented. I would also change how the government thinks about us, so that they can be able to see how hard working, and smart we are. I wanted to show that undocumented immigrants make this country better not worse. We come here for an opportunity for a better life, to be able to be a better person. All I ask for the laws is to have the opportunity for undocumented immigrants to be able to go to college and see who we really are and not being able to be judged from where we came but for who we are.

LIFE WILL GIVE YOU MORE THAN YOU EXPECT

Antonio Albizures-Lopez
Guatemala

Interviewed by: Jessica Pawlowski and India Young

When India and I interviewed Antonio we found out the true story, the background infor-mation of his life and it was very surprising. When we were telling the story he seemed very confident and proud of his life even though he was going through a hard time.

I never knew that my life would turn out this way. I am Guatemalan. I came from Guate-mala to the U.S. so my family and I can live a better life and to be raised in a better envi-ronment. My mother had traveled from Guatemala to this small state named Rhode Island on foot. She floated me on a tire across the river that is one of the most dangerous bodies of water and has taken millions of peoples' lives. My mother soon met up with my grand-mother where they then traveled to the U.S. together. My father tried to make it across the border but the first attempt was a failure and he was deported back to Guatemala. His second attempt was successful, and we were then able to live together happily.

My parents' goal was to leave the life of war, bloodshed, and death behind so that I could have a better life and be successful. My parents had worked hard to make a life for their sons. I went to school and struggled with the English language and getting good grades only to get to senior year of high school and find out that I could not go to college due to the fact that I am not an American citizen. In America the law is that people who are undocumented can't get financial aid and it makes it almost impossible for people who are undocumented to pay because the price becomes tripled. My brothers are lucky because they were born in this country. When my parents found out about this they were devastated because my parents gave up their hopes and dreams so that I could live a good life and be successful and they were just hurt to find out what this information was doing to me.

I faced so much depression and denial that eventually I looked at my whole life as a waste. I just didn't know what the point was of still proceeding on with school. Eventually after a while I got tired of slumping around, and I now work for an environmental group called Clear Water Action where we organize for environment and public health. My main motivation to get up and be something is my brothers. It feels good to know that they are able to go to school without difficulty and that just kind of influences me to do something.

Going through this experience made me look at everything as if it was meant to be. Everyone has a destiny, and things happen for me for a reason and this case this experi-ence just made me see that even though I can't go to school I can still make something out of myself. I hope that I can influence others who are going through the same thing I went through to go out and make something out of their lives even though they can't go to school.

LEAVING WAS NOT MY DECISION

Anonymous
Colombia
Interviewed by: Lynette Hernandez

I never thought I would be interviewing my own mother, asking her what her journey from Colombia to the United States was like but once I did I learned a lot about her that I would have never known if I had never asked.

Have you ever wondered what it's like to travel as a young child and leave all of your memories behind? I know someone that has had this experience just at the age of 9. She has never gone back to visit the place she was born in and this is her story.

I was about 8 or 9 when my family decided to move to the United States from Colombia. I never really thought about it when the thought came. My grandmother arranged for us to go to the United States to have a better life and I still have not yet been back to Colombia since I was 9, so it has been at least 27 years since I have visited my country. I would love to go see it now and how things have changed since I had been there and I would like the opportunity to go back and see where I grew up.

My journey here was much like how people travel today, by air plane. Traveling to a new country as a young child I didn't know what to expect when I got there. My biggest difficulties coming here were learning to speak English. It was really hard for me to accustom myself to the lifestyles of The United States because everything was different compared to Colombia. Typically my life as a child was really exciting because my father has 11 brothers and sisters in total and each of them had about four to five children. We all grew up together, always played together, always had family gatherings and we have always done everything together as a family. The journey we made was worth it because now I have a better life and better opportunities than I would have had being in Colombia. I appreciate coming here as a child even if leaving wasn't my decision.

A DIFFICULT PATH

Elda Duarte
Guatemala
Interviewed by: Jonathan Duarte

Interviewing my mother was really exciting. I got to hear many stories about where she lived when she was younger and what it was like living in a poor country. When my mom explained about leaving my sister in Guatemala, she cried for a little bit. But then, she went back to telling her story. My mom is old but she still has a good voice when it comes to telling stories.

I was so young and naïve back then. I came to the United States to prevent my family from starving to death. My family did not have enough money to eat or to drink, but when I was going to the United States, I thought I couldn't make it.

In Guatemala, my sister and I lived with our father. Together, with my sister and father, we worked in an agricultural field planting seeds of corn, beans, rice, tomato, watermelon and carrots onto the ground. Thanks to God, my father had land to farm or we would have had nothing. Sometimes, torrential rains would cause the seeds to rot or flow away. If there wasn't enough water, the drought would cause the plants to dehydrate, causing them to dry and shrivel up. If the entire harvest was destroyed, we would not have enough to eat or to sell to support our very existence. I was afraid that the harvest would be destroyed so I decided to cross the border to give a better future to my family.

When I made my way to the border of Mexico and Guatemala, I put my life at risk and asked "el coyote" to take me to the United States. ("El coyote" is a person who helps someone cross the border of Mexico). I thought that the journey to the United States was going to be a short one since I took the bus. My journey to the United States had just begun and I thought it was going to be a short and easy one. When the bus reached its destination, we were at Tapanatepec, Mexico. I heard some group of people on the bus that they were going to the United States just like me. That is when I thought I was going to make it to the United States in a few days, but when some of the people on the bus said that we weren't halfway there yet, I felt sad and disappointed. I wanted to go back to my country because of the long and unforgiving trip. I cried very quietly when suddenly a group of people helped me. During that moment they gave me their support and the confidence to move on because I paid a lot of money to go and I could not give up now. I felt glad that the group of people supported me. The people helped me and I helped them passing through many difficulties in the journey to the United States. After four weeks of traveling, I finally reached the border of the United States and Mexico and that was with the help of God and the people around me. I made it to the United States and I made myself set a goal to help my family in Guatemala.

It was because of my family that I decided to come to the United States for a better future. Thanks to God, my dream came true. My sister and my father are fine today thanks to my brave decision, and my daughter is here in the United States and shares her love with my family.

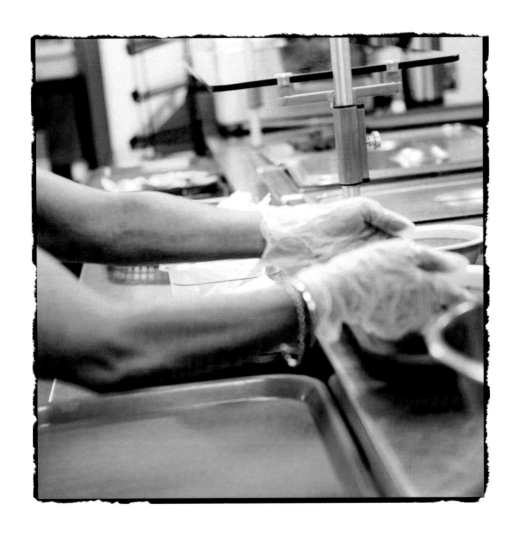

LIFE REALLY IS FULL OF SECOND CHANCES

Jader Velez
Colombia
Interviewed by: Juliana Velez

He was confused about what I was about to do. He begins to ask questions about what information I want, and where is this information going to appear. We were sitting at the dining table. He was wearing his soccer uniform and getting ready to go to the field. He wasn't emotional at all, but there was awkwardness while he thought of his past experiences.

"Can I turn back?" These are the thoughts that ran through my mind when I was already half way here. I was scared that I would get caught and get sent back to my country. However, the only goal I had in mind was to finish what I started. I know I'm risking my life, but it's hopefully going to be all worth it. In my head, life is always worth taking crazy risks, and this is definitely one of them.

This process took me about fifteen days. The day I left my house, my whole family brought me to the airport. Unfortunately, my mom wasn't there to say an official goodbye because she didn't have the strength to let me go. Seeing my whole family cry was heartbreaking. I was crying as well, but tears would never be a reason that would change my mind. My flights went in this order, from Colombia to Costa Rica, and from Costa Rica to Guatemala. It was in Guatemala that I began to walk. I crossed my first border from Guatemala to Mexico, and it was by far the worst experience I've ever had. Not only was I robbed by Coyotes, but my group and I got caught crossing the border from Guatemala to Mexico. We were all sent back to Guatemala, and my only option was to wait a week and try to cross again. We were all starving because all they offered us was beans. That was our meals for a full eight days, and it wasn't that tasty. In addition, thank God we had very good Coyotes crossing with us. They were always there to support us and help us accomplish our goal. While waiting in Mexico for two days, our Coyotes managed to get us in a very nice hotel until we left. When we left the hotel, we successfully crossed the second time, but we were robbed again by Coyote's before crossing from Mexico to the US.

There are many other challenges I didn't mention such as having to cross the two borders through rivers and deserts. It was a life risking experience, but I think it's all worth it. I have a wonderful wife and 3 beautiful daughters. I don't regret anything based on my experience. However, that was the last day I saw my mom. Never will I forget the sadness she had painted on her face before I left. I love her and miss her so much.

AN AMERICAN-CAPE VERDEAN

Suely Lima

Cape Verde

Interviewed by: Gina Nuñez

Interviewing Suely: Suely was wearing blue jeans and black jacket. She had a bright smile to her face. Her interview took place in a little room inside of Blackstone Academy where Suely expressed herself and told us her story!

I was born in Cape Verde and brought to the United States when I was eight years old, with my parents. I had a great experience on my way here. I was extremely happy to have my entire family by my side, my mother, father, sisters and my older brother. Coming to America I had no choice and made none of the decisions; my parents were the adults and they brought me here to America. It was hard at first when I had to adapt to the new language. I had no idea I would have to learn to speak English. Not knowing any English was my major struggle but eventually as I went to school I caught on. I can relate my struggles from the past to the struggles my parents still face today because they can not speak English well. I am the person who makes appointments for my parents and accompanies them to wherever they have to go.

Although I had no choice in coming here I value a lot coming with my whole family to the country. Bringing them with me is all I could've asked for. Growing up back in Cape Verde my life was not so bad; actually it was really good because my family didn't have a lot of struggles, and my parents were financially stable back in my home country. I really miss all the good memories I shared with my family back in Cape Verde. I wish I could've gone back to visit sooner and spend some time with my grandmother because she passed and I was not able to see her. Even though I visit Cape Verde I wish I could go back to visit sooner. Right now I go only about every 3 years because the economy here in the United States is not so good.

If I was ever to go back and live in Cape Verde it would be really hard because I am so used to the life here. It would be hard for me to know how to interact with a new life in Cape Verde because I've been in America practically my whole life. My journey to America was a wonderful experience. I have nothing bad to say about America because I know what my parents did was right and all they wanted to give me was the American dream; to be a successful person in life! I will be work hard towards giving my children a better financially stable life and the American dream as my parents gave to me.

I believe everyone should have equal rights, immigrant or not. A lot of young adults struggle to pursue a college education and have to pay out of state to tuition to attend because of their immigration status. If I could do something to help out I would help people look for ways to receive the right education, because I believe everyone deserves to be treated equal.

THE JOURNEY
Miriam Idarraga
Colombia
Interviewed by: Christian Montoya

Interviewing someone so close to me was very odd because I really didn't know how much trouble she had coming here. The most difficult thing interviewing someone so close was asking more and more questions because it felt uncomfortable

"Hey Miriam is that macaroni cheese done" Miriam "it's almost done". I currently work as a chef in a company that prepares food for the elderly and people with mental disadvantages. I am an American citizen; I became an American citizen April 10, 2008. I wake up around 5 in the morning, take shower, serve my husband and myself some cereal and go off to work. I live a happy life here in the USA even though I love my country which I do visit every year, I wouldn't live there because my life is here I have a house and a beautiful family.

In Colombia my family and I struggled a lot. We were 5 sisters, 6 brothers and 2 adopted sisters. My dad, my big brothers, and my sister and I had to take care of all of the family. It was very hard working to feed my family. Our family worked something out so that one person received higher education. My brother Fernando, did because he is the smartest. Even though we were poor we were the happiest family. I worked in a little supermarket and moved on to other jobs. I decided to come to the USA because I wasn't earning a lot of money and two of my brothers were already in the USA so I decided to go as well. I told my family they weren't happy but they knew it was the right decision. I borrowed the money from a cousin and planned on paying her back later on.

I paid the same coyote that got both of my brothers in. I was nervous. They told me I couldn't bring a lot of stuff, only one small bag. They bought the ticket from Bogota to Mexico City. From Mexico City I took a bus to a city near the Rio Bravo. The bus I went on was humid and crowded. When I got to that city we had to walk all the way to the Rio Bravo in foot. This was very hard I had to be sneaky but fast at the same time. When we arrived at the Rio Bravo I was scared, and I never stop praying to El Nino Jesus. The coyotes were always in a rush. We started to cross the Rio Bravo by swimming. I was drowning most of the time so the coyote grab me in something of rescue and helped me the rest of the way. The coyotes did all the paper work and I got a flight from LA to New York. From New York my cousin Luz Marina picked me up and I came to Rhode Island and lived the rest of my life.

DEAR GOD, WHY?

Anonymous
Mexico
Interviewed by: Juan Rodriquez

Happy life, steady job, and a loving family. Every thing seems happy, and it seems as though the rest of my life is going to go smoothly, with everything planned, no sudden changes. But that's just it, you can't plan life; reality likes to sneak up on you and bite you in the butt.

On October 11, 1998 my husband was caught in a crippling car wreck that left him a braindead husk who would hold on to life for another 7 years. Future torn asunder and torn to the ground I was rushed to America on a humanitarian visa. My husband was dying and they needed my presence in the country to keep him alive. Of course at the time I still regarded him as a living being. After all, it's only natural to want to be there for someone who only a couple of days before was a productive, responsive human being. It wasnt till much later when my kids arrived in America that I realized that my husband had died years ago in the wreck.... what was left was a shell of the soul that once inhabited the body, a breathing sarcophagus.... that wasn't my only trouble. Even having been here for 2 years I was still having difficulty fitting into America. Learning its language and finding a job that would hire an immigrant with no knowledge of the local customs. I thought our future was destroyed and that my kids and I would live a life of poverty and pain.

But that wasn't the case; my saving grace came in the form of the thing I was trying to protect and ensure the safety of my kids. They were young, impressionable, and they were learning fast. I took English classes for years and even then my English sounded like a stroke victim with a mouthful of peanut butter and a bad Spanish accent but my kids-they were grasping more than I ever could, every half hour just by watching what ever cartoon caught their fancy on tv. The fact that they could translate complex issues to me helped me stay afloat until I got some control of my situation.... until now.

Today I'm doing okay, I have a nice car, I live in a nice neighborhood.... well at least nice for Central Falls, and my financial situation is no longer hopeless. What I'm trying to say is hope is there, the dream is still alive but since so many are already here looking for it, it's going to take some searching to find it, so don't lose hope.

.

I CANNOT AND WILL NOT COMPLAIN

Sonn Sam
America

This story is not an interview, it is a This I Believe essay written for NPR. Sonn Sam, the son of Sokhon, wrote this, his personal mantra, and we believe it to be a great place to end this book.

His name was Samdang Sam and he was my brother. He died of starvation a little before his second birthday. I never met him, but he's probably the person who has most impacted my life.

My mother always had unique - and often creative - ways for disciplining me. She followed the tradition of strict and harsh discipline such as physical beatings, found in most Cambodian households, with horrific stories of the struggles she and my father endured to make it to America. My parents are survivors of one the most gruesome genocides known to man. Approximately two million people were brutally murdered in Cambodia by the Khmer Rouge, a communist regime led by Pol Pot. Once Pot was in power and gained control of Cambodia, my parents and Samdang, like all of the other citizens, were forced into a life of slavery.

They were sent to labor camps and their sole purpose was to harvest rice that fed the regime. My parents were led to work at sun-up and my brother was given to caretakers in the camp. I use the term caretakers loosely because care meant leaving the kids of the camp in a fenced area, guarded by soldiers of the Khmer Rouge, to wait for their parents. If they were disrespectful or fought amongst themselves, they were immediately executed. My mother told me how she cried every waking moment, not from working like a mule in the rice fields, being whipped and beaten for resting because of exhaustion, or being fed one spoon of rice a day, but from the fear that she might not see her child when she returned.

Samdang was an energetic and playful child. My mother spoke of how he always smiled, even in the midst of the tragedy that unfolded. However, as time passed his playfulness and smiles dissipated because he just didn't have the energy. Needless to say, one spoonful of rice is nowhere nutritionally adequate for grown adults, let alone a developing infant. He grew weaker and weaker.

One story in particular that my mother shared stuck with me. One day my father was working in the rice fields and by accident stepped on a baby crab. He immediately used his weight to hold it captive until the coast was clear for him to reach down and grab it. My father tucked the crab in the inner lining of his pant uniform and continued to work. Once he returned to the camp, he waited until nightfall to make his move. There were bon fires ignited throughout the camp and my father walked by one, threw the crab in, and came back for it a few minutes later. He then returned to Samdang with this crab, it's shell burnt to a crisp, but with the meat cooked enough to eat. My mother explained how hard it was for them to see their weak child slowly eat this small crab while they, too, were starving. Shortly after, Samdang died in my mother's arms.

I don't know if she knew at the time, or even realizes today, how this story continues to directly and indirectly guide how I live my life. Through her stories I learned the meaning of sacrifice, courage, and love. I learned that I have absolutely nothing to complain about and everything to appreciate. I cannot and will not complain because complaining focuses only on the negative, and my parents taught me that their survival depended on their optimism and the fierce fighting spirit of love for their family. I cannot and will not complain because I've learned that the true measure of human worthiness is not what we gain, but in the sacrifices we are willing to make for the people we love and the ideals we believe. I cannot and will not complain because I come from strong and proud people who through the worst time in their history maintained their identity, their culture, and their overwhelming love for life. I cannot and will not complain because I am the next generation of a great family that passed on their hopes, dreams, vision, and strength to me so their loving spirit may survive for many years to come, and serve as a clear and shining example of human dignity and character.

Most importantly, I cannot and will never complain or ever take anything in my life for granted because until his last moment my brother never did.

THE INTERVIEWERS

Immigration Project Class 2007-2008

(Left to Right) Front: Priscilla McPhillips, Jacki Cano, Angela Boror, Patricia Delgado, Lorraine Vergara, Melanie Gonzalez, Merari Lima, Carolina Rosario, Brianda Franco.
(Left to Right) Back: Carlos Gonzalez, Maria Benoit, Stephany Restrepo, Gina Nuñez, Melissa Montoya, Ali Baptista, Deborah Reyes, Stacy Joslin, Jaryde Spencer-Santos

Immigration Project Class 2009-2010

(Left to Right) Front: Juliana Velez, Tatiana Reis, Stephany Restrepo, Jacki Cano, Gina Nuñez, Jessica Pawlowski, Lynette Hernandez
(Left to Right) Back: Paola Arroyo, Christian Montoya, Sebastian Osorio, India Young, Adelsandra Lopes, Juan Rodriguez, Brittany Ortiz
Missing from Photo: Diana Giraldo, Cristian Giraldo, & Jonathan Duarte